BLUE SONOMA

✽

BLUE SONOMA

Jane Munro

BRICK BOOKS

LIBRARY AND ARCHIVES CANADA CATALOGUING IN PUBLICATION

Munro, Jane, 1943-, author
    Blue sonoma / Jane Munro.

Poems.
ISBN 978-1-926829-88-3 (pbk.)

    I. Title.

PS8576.U574B58 2014 C811'.54 C2013-907366-3

Copyright © Jane Munro 2014.

We acknowledge the Canada Council for the Arts, the Government of Canada through the Canada Book Fund, and the Ontario Arts Council for their support of our publishing program.

 Canada Council for the Arts / Conseil des Arts du Canada  Government of Canada / Gouvernement du Canada  ONTARIO ARTS COUNCIL / CONSEIL DES ARTS DE L'ONTARIO

The author photo was taken by Marlis Funk.

This book is set in Adobe Garamond Pro, a digital interpretation of the roman types of Claude Garamond and the italic types of Robert Granjon, designed by Robert Slimbach and released in 1989.

Cover image, design and layout by Cheryl Dipede.
Printed and bound by Sunville Printco Inc.

Brick Books
431 Boler Road, Box 20081
London, Ontario N6K 4G6
www.brickbooks.ca

Om
purnamadah purnamidam
purnat purnamudachyate
purnasya purnamadaya
purnameva vashishyate
Om shanti, shanti, shanti

All this is full. All that is full.
From fullness, fullness comes.
When fullness is taken from fullness,
Fullness still remains.

Invocation to the *Isha Upanishad*

❖

CONTENTS

SONOMA　13

DARKLING

1　17
2　18
3　19
4　20
5　21
6　22
7　23
8　24
9　25
10　26
11　27
12　28

DREAM POEMS

The net of heaven is cast wide　31
There is a frog　32
Grenade with its red pin　33
I was on a bus　34
His upper arms are marked　35
In a small boat off Port Renfrew　36
Moonlight falls between the trees　37
He stops her on the trail　38
A poet is walking the platform　39
The boat that was not a boat　40
It was a dry-weave hiker's undershirt　41
A pool clear as tea　42

OLD MAN VACANAS

1. 45
2. 46
3. 47
4. 48
5. 49
6. 50
7. 51
8. 52
9. 53
10. 54
11. 55

SUTRA

The live arbutus carries dead branches   59
In the drift towards sleep, a green face   60
Beauty the mediating principle, the moon said   61
The house is dark   62
A small doll nested in hollow dolls   63
My mind is my grandchild   64
"Lao Tzu" also has the meaning of "old man"   65
Hard to find space   66
So you come   67
Mine me   68
In the slow spin of stars, a dancer turns   69

VALLEY OF THE MOON   73

NOTES   75
ACKNOWLEDGEMENTS   77
ABOUT THE AUTHOR   79

*

Sonoma

He totalled his blue truck –
slowly spun out on an icy bridge,
rammed it into a guard rail.

Climbed out unbruised.
Coal Creek. Middle of nowhere.
A passing couple brought him home.

Then three years
with letters from the Motor Vehicle Department
before he relinquished his license.

Before we met, while driving cab,
he broke his neck. It rewelded
off-kilter: head stuck forward.

Six years later, it's that jut I suddenly see ahead.
It's late, but for once no mist or fog. And on all
the twists and turns of that coastal highway,

its bluffs and coves, I am following
the spitting image of him
in that battered Sonoma –

its peeling paint, cracked brake lens,
the slumped driver silhouetted by my lights –
only the two of us on the road.

DARKLING

1

This is what I remember of life:
the glans of a penis, smooth as an acorn,

split like a cat's eye with a vertical pupil.
Weeping pearly tears.

On a salmonberry, the swollen drupelets
quilting its surface with peachy clitorises.

Words like frogs, their sudden leaps
and pulsing, thin-skinned bodies.

The singing when we stopped to listen.

2

And this: dying is not a plot solution.
It doesn't resolve character flaws.

Froth on her lip flecked with blood.
Wind rolling air's opals across the beach.

Peeling the grape of death.
That love would feed you this.

3

The eyes of a monkey. Rhesus amber eyes.
Intention sealed in murky sclera.

Moon-snail shells: whorled breasts.
Owl's silence on a branch.

The monkey's small sharp teeth.
His mother's stomach flattening as she nursed him.

The whites of our eyes. Giving us away.
Infant following a mother's gaze.

Sun shades along the ghat. Beads recited.
Thread across a young man's chest. Sutras chewed upon.

4

Mullions and muntins: true divided lights. Windows
lit from inside cast rhomboids on the roof.

Merton's phrase: *Humility against despair.*
A hope so small I could have swallowed it –

a ball of opium as she stepped into the flames.
His match-stick body crisscrossed when he fell.

A nurse probed the wound bed with a steel skewer.
Maggots cleaned out the abscess, then ate each other.

Merton electrocuted accidentally in Thailand.
Something wonky in the wiring.

5

Hawthorn. Huckleberry. Rain on
magnolia petals.

Under the arbutus, miniature urns
and the scent of honey.

Under the cherry, pink mulch.
Girls braiding streamers; skipping this way,

that way, over and under,
laying a plait. May Day practice.

Hands that bled from the thorns. My friend's
mother's wedding bouquet of hawthorn blossoms.

6

The man with the gift of divining. In the green light
of his X-ray cabinet, shoes too tight.

That third Benedictine vow:
Obedience. Stability. *Conversatio morum.*

Walls and floors appeared where forests lived.
Babies pulled themselves up on coffee tables.

Elephants culled for destroying habitat.
Matriarch leading her family across years of drought.

7

The stone that made me think of a full soul
smooth and heavy in my hand. Slightly freckled.

A wooden house. A couple at a wooden table.
The cleverness of fitted bones. Skin bags of gewgaws.

That next room which I could enter, or not.
The curtain to be parted.

8

Climbing metal staircases in the library stacks.
A hole carved through my chest, stuffed

with that bouquet of roses he gave me
the day I couldn't stop crying. Stems

as long as broomsticks behind my back,
colliding with pillars, smashing into things.

9

A candle guttering. Branches rising and lowering
just slightly, the way his chest did.

Day drawing its skirts up, stepping across the strait.
The rustle of petticoats over stones

and then, tweed – a heavy overcoat.
Flash of satin lining.

The times I studied him:
surely, surely, he wasn't empty of himself. Not yet.

10

Inner steel that's flexible, outer layers hard –
sharpened to a five-body edge.

Quenched in a trough of water,
the blade curved into an arc

strong as a spider's web,
blousy in a breeze. Tough as a virus.

Able to pass through another body
if need be.

11

The row of silent houses – places where life went on.
Wind pouring down the slopes, curling up

as it hits their structures. Tides of cold air.
Slowly, the plain is moving.

The pleated, deeply wrinkled brain – the crumpled former seabed.
A row of unpainted shacks. Snow-dusted foothills.

12

Mallard above. Mallard below. Two green, iridescent necks, one reaching up, one down. Two curls on two tails.

And us, were we substance or reflection?
Moon boat sailing high.

DREAM POEMS

�

The net of heaven is cast wide

and I look up
at a frond of glittering white mesh

in wonder, and speak to a man
standing at the rail beside me
and hear him say,

This is all ours now.
We can't go back.

We drift through ferns
white as the frost on windowpanes.

There are others
but we haven't been talking.

He is not a person I knew in life.

There is a frog

in one piston
of a crankcase.
It has the power to clean
the chamber
in which it hibernates.
It eats in its sleep, delicately
scraping the walls
with its feet.
I feel it kick in me.

Grenade with its red pin

beside perfume bottles
on the bathroom counter.

He said, *Do it.*
I did; we ran.

He broke a trail uphill
through deep snow.

We waited on a bluff above the house.
The explosion did not come.

A man in a suit and tie
drove up in a car.

I was on a bus

for a long ride –
the Lions Gate Bridge
(a conveyor belt),
the North Shore Mountains
(loaves of bread).

I was tired. I made a bed
on the back bench. In the aisle
there was a bucket of water
and floating in it
a doll's fancy dress, no more
than twelve inches long. It seemed
that someone was inside, but, no –
it was only a dress. A lanky man
ogled it and smacked his lips.
What have we here?

His upper arms are marked

with red Xs.
He has to sit in the solution
for some time.

The basin is porcelain.
He's not chained
but might as well be.

Or locked in wooden stocks
in a square by the town pump.
This is a sentence

he cannot correct.
What he thought was him
were clouds dissolving.

In a small boat off Port Renfrew

a woman trolling for halibut
caught the moon.

It was pale and pocked.
It lengthened from disc to oval to flatfish
as she lifted it. The rod bowed.

When the rod's tip touched the water's surface
the moon sprang from the waves
streaming foam, and soared overhead.

The woman fell on her back –
winded, wordless – rocking as the boat rocked.
The moon hung above her,
huge and closer than a star.

It had grown on a tongue of silt
at the river's mouth, dark-side-down,
resting on its mind-reading side,
then slid to deep waters.

Staring up at it, the woman knew it knew.

Moonlight falls between the trees

Its white railings surround
the dead, who stand out of our ken.

A voice spoke her name and woke her.

The moon is the breast of a young woman
bending down behind a tall fir.

She took the bag of bones and flew
off into the night.
It was a string bag. A green string bag.
She flew the way an eagle flies,
carrying a dangling animal.
They were the bones from a man, but not
boiled white bones.
It was prudent to gather them up.

The railings of moonlight
drop across grass.
The dead press against them, a forest
of shadows uphill from the house,
crossing creek beds and mountain ranges.

A young woman's breast
without the darkened nipple and aureole
of a mother. A breast still close
to the curve of chest, not pulled
by feeding. A hunting breast,
out with her owls.

She was taking the bones
into the deepest dark of the forest
and leaving them someplace lost.
That man was going to be all gone.
She was doing what needed to be done.

He stops her on the trail

and asks, *Where are you going?*
He's the new owner.
His beach is a nice place to pee –
squat and look out
at the small island, the mountains
across the strait.
He appears
to want to start things off on the right foot,
but she knows where his property lines lie
and how frequently
she transgresses them.
Still, when he asks she says *tea*
and sits on his couch, meets his wife and his daughter,
who's been swimming in the ocean.
It's very cold. The girl must be a seal.
They are all more dangerous than she imagined.
The next day
he's between her and her kitchen.
They circle each other, hackles up,
and she breaks for the house – but he's on the step.
She bashes him in the face,
bag splitting, green beans spilling over his shoulders.
He's a coon come to the porch
to stand on hind legs, paw the glass
when she slams the door.
So it's time
to take that plunge,
disappear –
go without thought.

A poet is walking the platform

of an underground station, holding
a sign that says "German lessons."
She's wearing a blue dress.
Later, she's carrying a sign that says
"Kissing lessons."

Upstairs, the streets are flooded
and gas leaks bubble through the city's tailings.
Pavement is breaking up
the way sea ice melts, chunks
jamming together. Poets everywhere –
a bloom of poets. In the snarl
of bitter currents, even salmon
can't taste their way home.

The boat that was not a boat

cruised on pavement –
carried its load of passengers down
into the deepest parking lot.
The boat was a slow-moving trolley
with seats along each side.
There were few sights –
just cars and more cars.
We rode at the pace of royalty.
As if we'd built a cathedral.
As if flying buttresses and a rose
window would loft from earth's bowels.
Now and then the driver paused
and we fell silent, observing shadowed
and slightly shimmering Fords,
GMCs, Hondas, Saabs, Peugeots, Toyotas
in which we drove to work,
carried potting soil, ferried
dogs and children, stored reusable grocery bags
and flats of spring water, transported those much-desired
presents in their impenetrable packaging.

It was a dry-weave hiker's undershirt

he never took off.
Embedded at the nape of the neck
were three flat, green worms
fossilized into the fabric.

He did not like change, but kept
moving through range after range,
a backwoods man
we hardly saw, elusive as the albino bear.

When we found him,
even the wool of his sweater was thin.
We unpeeled him clinically
as if he were mummified –
2000 years old – but it was only him, the one
we'd believed to be there all along,
though we had come to recognize
how long he'd been missing.

A pool clear as tea

in which the submerged
bird is visible
as the ferns and mossy rocks beside it,
the fallen trees with their arching branches –
and my hope
that the bird will finish its rooting underwater
and rise.
There is only so long it can stay down.
It has to breathe. I am also
holding my breath, watching.
But when it lifts its head
the bird staring at me is not a heron.
It is not even a duck or a grebe.
It is an owl.
Dark holes in widening circles –
its eyes.

OLD MAN VACANAS

✻

1

The old man
to whom I'm married
hits the sack again
after breakfast.

A black bear
out in the rain
on Blueberry Flats.

Is it too wet
to hibernate? The muddy creek
burgeoning.

By lunch, he's up.
The sky's no lighter – candles
with our tea.

Tell me, can a soul
fatten up for winter?

2

The old man
who works in the garden
grows garlic.

He asks what day it is.
Hail falls.
On every bent leaf, a load
of pearls.
His calendar melts,
its pages slipping into soil.
Bulbs wrap their cloven shoulders
in scraps of tissue paper.

Daffodils
cuffed by squalls
spill scent.
Stout garlic
defends its yard.

None of this matters to him
any more than greying hair.

3

A fire on the hearth, lantern by the bed,
kitchen candelabra in a draft.
Finger of light on an arm of the bench.
One of the cats watching it beckon.

We have met the lion of March.
Today, her tongue abrades my back.

Outside, excuses pile up.
Snow like lamb's wool
sliding down windows.
Posts with stockings about their ankles.

I tuck my hands into my sleeves.
Ravens carry twigs
to their nest in a double-headed cedar.
We who are paired. Even his lips are cold.
Thanks to beams and rafters,
the house becomes a whale.

The miles of intestines facing Jonah.

4

The old man
losing his mind
registers
the weather systems
of intelligence.

Climate change, for all
its extinctions,
won't alter the planet's orbit.

Our laundry tossing,
turning the clearing for a morning
into a ship.

Light billowing through wet sheets.

5

The old man who picks up the phone
does not get your message.

Call again.
Please call again.

The cats leave squirrel guts
on the Tibetan rug.
Augury I cannot read.

You've got to talk with me.

I scrape glistening coils
into a dust pan,
spit on drops of blood and spray ammonia.
The blood spreads into the white wool.

I am so sick of purring beasts.

Don't tempt me, old man.
Today I have four arms
and weapons in each hand.

6

If you want to know the way
out here,
I'll tell you.

Drive and drive.
The road goes up and down, to and fro.

If you want to come visit,
I'll invite you.

My old man won't know
the difference
between you and billy-be-damned.

He's been wearing out old thoughts—
holes now in plenty.
Fewer in his drawers.
And he's not keen on new ones.

We lay the bricks of conversation.
Block one. Block two.
Small. Tidy.
Start again.
Solid. Reassuring.
Four windowless walls.

Roar up the drive. Spit gravel. Blow your horn.

I am gnawing through myself.

7

Doe on the driveway
with this year's fawn
and last year's, now full grown,
eating salmonberry leaves.

Carrying the mail, I walk past.
The deer go on browsing.

My old man
likes magazines. He stands
at the cutting board, leafing through
today's haul. Turns cartoons
in my direction.

Rural postbox half a mile away:
how I keep an eye on the neighbourhood.

Who's laughing at us today?
Fools set in our ways.

8

My old man
oh, my old man, oh my
old man

is lean
as a wooden spoon
stirring batter
that folds
around it the way
at his waist
a softness drapes.

He sleeps on his back,
straight as a broom.
He sleeps on his side,
curled like a cat.
He sleeps with the heater going
and a T-shirt on.
My old man likes
to catch some zzzzzzzs.

9

Now this old man
has ripened sweetly.

He gazes at me,
bemused and happy.

On his way to the sink
he bops the empty coffee pot
on my crown.

10

The old man
feeding the fire
keeps us primitive.

Dark falling early.
A few sticks in flames
snap their fingers—come,
move your stumps!

The old man pokes at them.
Sparks scatter.

Pull up a chair. Have some wine.
Be our guest.

11

The old man
takes his choppers out
when chicken sticks to them.

He parks them in a glass
of blue fizz.

DNA from fossil bones
tells us we're siblings to Neanderthals—

and the small arrangements
we make? Language, travel, art? Props

in a little, local, theatre of light.

SUTRA

✽

The live arbutus carries dead branches

grey wood twisted tight
within the framework of the tree –
impossible to snap off,
forged as it dries.

And in me, parts I can't imagine
myself without – silvering.

Healthy branches flower.
Rufous hummingbirds arrive.
Berries hang in clusters, fall.
Strips of papery ochre skin peel away
from the smooth green muscle
of spreading limbs.

But I know what lasts.
What claims each twig is hard
to carve into spoons or boxes,
or burn.

How gracefully the tree
holds up these swords
among its branches.

In the drift towards sleep, a green face

with eyes carved through its jade, alive as rivers are alive.

The bridge shuddering. Slate-coloured eddies about pillars.
No other route into town.

Get it straight, kiddo. No expectations, no losses.
That face is afloat.

Beauty the mediating principle, the moon said

between goodness and severity.

Her spinning wheel sounds like a coffee grinder
but steadier. So she's working today. Any news of my fate?

But it shuts off: that was a shower. Pipes clanked
at its closing. He said the diagnosis was like

stepping into an elevator
and finding nothing there – no floor beneath him.

The house is dark

We walk toward it
with a flashlight.
We walk slowly.
He has his cane in one hand.
The other floats and grabs, reaching
for my shoulder as his footing
tilts on gravel and ruts.
He is looking down, back hunched
and neck crooked.
I lift the beam. Windows glimmer.
Porch and door. Roof lines.
More windows, then higher up –
his study. Mine. Chimneys. Home.
It's going to be here when he's gone.
A sob catches in his throat. He's trembling.
Again, with the flashlight,
I show him the house. We stand there
silent in the dark, and look
at where we've dwelt.

A small doll nested in hollow dolls

sits on a shelf
in a house on a street in a city on earth
in a solar system fitted into the milky way
that rides on the blooming universe

but where is all this

water knows to be water
a spruce grows into a spruce
in a crevice
buckling down, living on less

grasping the entire address can't matter

mountain
topped with a temple
whose god has a pleasing countenance, a broken tusk
and four arms
and is tended by a family
under the same roof as their cows

incomprehensibly
all this is, all that is
itself
translated over and over
present at any address

My mind is my grandchild

We sit on the beach,
my arms and legs about him.
He rests against me. I feel
his curls under my chin.
We watch the waves.
We watch light on the waves –
its quick crowd,
passengers changing trains.
We listen.

His anxiety comes and goes.
He speaks of it, asking,
Is it time? When?

He is a good boy
and sits still.
I hope he will absorb this beach.
I hope it will stay with him.

Then, coming down the green steps,
loaded with his baby sister –
his mom, his dad.

Can my mind unlearn
anxiety? Attend to
what is – and what will
continue to be here long after
my mind?

"Lao Tzu" also has the meaning of "old man"

It's time —
let the wild mother
who builds a blue fire in the belly
stand tall,
let flames flow, electric
inside and outside the skin,
let blue tongues lick
a bird body
whose wings fountain blue.
Give this one full sway,

then invite home
the father who throws
windows open in the head,
loads its squatters on flying carpets:
a flock of dwindling figures sent sailing away.
Welcome this one
and summer's full flush.

When the will wakes up,
let it eat fruit.
Sit a while and watch.

Sometime, it too may
get to be
an old man.

Hard to find space

in the nitty-gritty
of a city running on time.

Old woman, Eros can arise
and go now beyond bean rows
and the hive for the honey bee.

It's only a cabin I've built here.

Traffic of red blood cells –
heart coursing with cyclists
pedaling in long skirts,
baskets on their bikes.

I'm bringing home a baguette
baked at five a.m.

Will you break bread with me?

So you come

stinking to high heaven
with all the foulness
of your worn-out stories –
je me souviens.
Bunions. Spittle. Squint.

You have yet to crack a smile,
your eyes wind tunnels.

And maybe you're what I get –
the rush to destruction,
that whistling maw.
Eros exiled.

Bloody Time, you old cannibal
with your necklace of skulls.

By the scruff of your neck
I hoist you – toss you out.
Hose you down.
Drenched, you glitter.

Now,
in my arms,
in your nightgown,
you're just an old woman –
frail, beset, bedraggled –
familiar as my kitchen.
How long for this world?

I reinsert you in the captain's chair.
Across the table
we take each other in.

You tear off a chunk of baguette,
toss it my way.
Got your goat, eh?

Mine me

not for fuel –
drill for diamonds.

Varicose veins of kimberlite
with its pipes from karmic volcanoes.

Facet knobby rocks, shape prisms –
make the sharpest blade.

In the slow spin of stars, a dancer turns

He wears a tall hat. His arms stretch –
one out, one up. His robes flow.

In the slow spin of stars, a woman sings.
Her voice floats on her breath.
She opens her mouth and words emerge.

In the slow spin of stars, a boat glides.
It rides the currents.
It is made of glass. It carries the sun.

In the slow spin of stars, a yellow dog
lies on the pavement, her nose in her groin.
She is a bitch, a cur. She has tits and pups.

In the slow spin of stars, a tree grows.
Its branches curl up and are wrapped
by two vines. It's a pillar of greenery.

In the slow spin of stars, crystals form.
All the elemental glyphs.
Alphabets.

❈

Valley of the Moon

On the drive to the respite hotel,
the *Goldberg Variations*: a bridge to peace.

Sora bidding farewell to Bashō –
Sora leaning forward on his elbow.

      *

In the moment of leaving,
when words set sail from paper . . .

soul clings
to one burning
as fire clings to a stick.

      *

Even when the mind's a sieve,
soul doesn't grieve –
cannot believe

in scarcity. A mountain,
a river – fully this,
fully that.

NOTES

The epigraph is Eknath Easwaran's translation of a Sanskrit prayer (sometimes called the "Peace Invocation") used as the invocation to the *Isha Upanishad*.

P.13: "Sonoma," the brand name of a line of GMC compact pickup trucks, is the name of a Californian county. According to Jack London, who had a ranch there, "Sonoma" derives from a Miwok word meaning "Valley of the Moon" – the title of one of his novels – but this is disputed. It could also mean "many moons" or, if it comes from another language, it might refer to "earth village" or even "nose."

P. 20: Thomas Merton's phrase, "Humility against despair," is a chapter heading in his book of essays, *New Seeds of Contemplation*.

P.22: Trappists follow the Rule of St. Benedict; the vow of *conversatio morum* is a commitment to on-going transformation of self.

P. 26: Legendary *katana* (Samurai swords) were capable of slicing through a row of warriors at one swoop. Their sharpness was reputedly tested on the bodies of convicted criminals. Some museum pieces are rated as having a "five-body" edge.

P.43: Vacanas are colloquial prayer poems. Addressed to the poet's personal deity, they draw their imagery from nature and domestic activities. In the original Kannada, *vacana* means "saying; thing said." Although this is a form used with sophistication by yogi-philosophers – including the extraordinary woman, Mahadeviyakka – in twelfth-century South India the verse is not aureate; it remains frank, accessible and striking.

ACKNOWLEDGEMENTS

Thanks to the editors of *The Malahat Review* and *The Fiddlehead* where earlier versions of some of these poems were first published.

An earlier version of "Darkling" ("This is what I remember of life on earth") received Honourable Mention in *The Malahat Review*'s 2011 Long Poem competition.

"The boat that was not a boat," first published in *The Fiddlehead*, is included in *Best Canadian Poetry in English 2013*, (Tightrope Books, Barrie ON). Thanks to Sue Goyette, editor of the 2013 anthology, and to Molly Peacock, the series editor.

My sincere thanks to the Canada Council for the Arts for a Grant to Professional Writers, to the British Columbia Arts Council for a Project Grant in Creative Writing, to the Banff Centre for the Arts for funding to attend the 2011 Writing Studio, to Access Copyright for a Professional Development Grant, and to the Saskatchewan Writers' Guild for their subsidized Artists and Writers' Colonies.

Many thanks to the Brick Books team: Barry Dempster, Alayna Munce, Sue Sinclair, Nick Thran, Cheryl Dipede, the inimitable Kitty Lewis, and my wonderful editor, Don McKay. I am also grateful to Carolyn Forché and John Barton; Marilyn Bowering, Jan Conn, Rebeca Helfer and Ian Munro; Lorna Crozier and my fellow colonists at St. Pete's; Roo Borson for serving as a sounding board; and Jan Zwicky for her insights and friendship.

Blue Sonoma is in memory of Robert Amussen, 1924 – 2013.

Jane Munro is the author of five previous books of poetry, most recently *Active Pass* (Pedlar Press, 2010) and *Point No Point* (McClelland & Stewart, 2006). Her work has received the Bliss Carman Poetry Award and the Macmillan Prize for Poetry, and has been nominated for the Pat Lowther Award. She is a member of Yoko's Dogs (Jan Conn, Mary di Michele, Susan Gillis, Jane Munro), a poetry collective whose first book, *Whisk* (Pedlar Press), was published in 2013. After living for twenty years on the coast of Vancouver Island, she has now returned to Vancouver.